FAMILY REUN

The Preens
of
Leebotwood

Susan Laflin

ISBN 978-1-326-16619-9

Acknowledgements

My thanks to all those who provided the pictures and information used in this booklet and especially to Angela Clarke, Joan Davies, Pauline Davies, Philip Davies, Ann Hone, Fred Medlicott, John Millward, Jane Taylor, Patricia Theobald, Mary Thomas and Mary Wilson.

Published by The Preen Family History Study Group
www.preen.org.uk

Cover photograph: Leebotwood church.

CONTENTS

CHAPTER ONE: INTRODUCTION 5

    1.1 BACKGROUND 5

CHAPTER TWO: RICHARD PREEN 1807-1887 7

CHAPTER THREE: HIS CHILDREN & GRANDCHILDREN ... 11

    3.1 WILLIAM PREEN 1842-1879 11

    3.2 ANNIE HUGHES (BORN PREEN) 1844-1931 12

        Arthur John Hughes 1868-? 15

        Edith Sarah Hughes later Hinksman 1870-1923 16

        Elizabeth Hughes 1876-? 16

        Annie Gertrude Hughes 1878-1966 17

        Mary Emily Hughes 1879-? 17

        Christopher Charles Hughes 1881-1953 17

        Elizabeth Mabel Grace Hughes, later Downes 1882-? 18

        Frances Dora Hughes 1886-1979 18

    3.3 JAMES PREEN 1846- 1927 18

        William Preen 1874-1957 20

    3.4 MARY MEDLICOTT (BORN PREEN) 1848 - 1908 20

        Mary Preen Medlicott, later Jarvis 1872-? 22

        Arthur John Medlicott 1876-? 22

    3.5 JOHN PREEN 1851-1929 23

    3.6 RICHARD PREEN 1854-1925 24

        Annie Lilian Preen, later Williams 1881-? 26

        Elizabeth Emily Preen, later Monk 1883-? 26

        Frederick William Preen 1885-1955 27

        Edith Martha Preen 1887-1969 27

        Albert Cecil Preen 1891-? 27

    3.7 SAMUEL PREEN 1856 - 1938 28

        Arthur Frank Preen 1890-1960 32

        Agnes Annie Preen 1891-1984 33

        Edith Nellie Preen 1894-1926 34

CHAPTER FOUR: THE 2012 FAMILY REUNION 35

Chapter One: Introduction

The Preen Family History Study group exists to study the history of this family and organises an annual reunion each June. In 2012 they met in Leebotwood.

DNA Analysis has shown that the PREEN family is divided into three main groups. The Cardington Group is probably descended from Philip and Mary Preen who lived in Hope Bowdler during the seventeenth century (1660 onwards).

One of their descendants was Richard Preen (1807-1887) who married Sarah King and settled in Leebotwood, where he ran the village shop, managed the coal mine and farmed. His family continued there until 1984 when his last grand-daughter died of old age.

1.1 Background

We believe that the PREEN family took their name from the Domesday manor of Prene which lies in Shropshire, just north of Much Wenlock and Wenlock Edge. This family originated in the West Midlands of England and spread throughout the world, but remained most common in Shropshire and Gloucestershire.

The early records of the fifteenth and sixteenth centuries show some of them living either in Hope Bowdler (a small parish close to Church Stretton among the hills of south Shropshire). The history of the Preen Family may be seen on our website *www.preen.org.uk*

The Cardington group moved from Hope Bowdler to the next parish of Cardington around 1790. One of their members was John Preen who married Hannah Gallear and settled at Cardington Hill. They had four sons, each of whom had a large family. The youngest of these was Richard Preen who moved to Leebotwood. The map on the next page shows places in Shropshire associated with this family.

SMETHCOTT

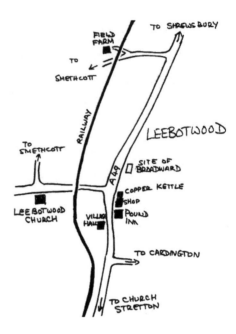

Chapter Two: Richard Preen 1807-1887

Richard Preen was the youngest son of John Preen and Hannah (formerly Gallear) and was baptised in Cardington in June 1807.

```
                      |-William Preen 1841-1841
                      |-William Preen 1842-1879
                      |-Anne Preen 1844-?
                      |        mar 1867  ------------------------- 8 children
                      | Christopher Hughes
                      |-James Preen 1846-1927
Richard Preen         |        mar 1871 ------------------------- 4 children
1807-1887             | Eliza Jones
     mar c1840 ---- |-Mary Preen 1848-1908
Sarah King            |        mar 1868 ------------------------ 4 children
c1816-1881            | William Medlicott
                      |-John Preen 1851-1929
                      |-Richard Preen 1854-1925
                      |        mar 1880 ------------------------ 6 children
                      | Martha Cheesbrough
                      |-Samuel Preen 1856 - 1938
                      |        mar 1888  ----------------------- 3 children
                      | Ellen Matthews
```

On 26th October 1840, **Richard Preen** ("shoemaker") and **Sarah King** ("servant") were married in St Chads church, Shrewsbury. They both gave "New Street" as their place of residence, Richard was the son of John Preen, stonemason and Sarah the daughter of William King, labourer.

The baptisms of Richard's first two sons in 1841 and 1842 show that he was living at Enchmarsh in Cardington and working as a shoemaker.

His daughter Anne was baptised in Leebotwood on 21st July 1844 when Richard was described as a shopkeeper. Her baptism was followed by those of James (10th September 1846) and Mary (17th September 1848).

The 1851 census showed the whole family in the same household and Richard gave his profession as "grocer". Volume VIII of the

The Pound Inn, Leebotwood.

Victoria County History of Shropshire says that *"The village shop, adjoining the Pound Inn, is first recorded in 1851. Until c1917 it was occupied by the Preen family, who also leased the colliery c1863-75, and were coal-merchants until c1905. A carpenter and a shoemaker had gone out of business by 1895."*

However Richard was described as "shopkeeper" in 1844, suggesting that the shop actually started a few years earlier. Richard was also described as "shopkeeper" in the baptisms of his three younger children, John (25th December 1851), Richard (5th February 1854) and Samuel (26th July 1856).

Volume VIII of the Victoria County History of Shropshire says: *"Leebotwood colliery was opened in 1784 and its original workings were only a few yards from the houses on Padmore Lane. After 1804 the pits lay nearer to the main road, east of the line of the railway. In 1832, 13 cottages in Leebotwood were occupied by colliers. Fields Farm, which stands on the site of the house occupied by the lessee of the colliery in 1784, was rebuilt in brick shortly before 1832."*

" .... the establishment of Leebotwood colliery in 1784. The colliery was normally leased, the lord of the manor receiving royalties, and was held by tenants until 1808. ..... between 1831 & 1834 it was operated by the lord of the manor under a manager. .... but Richard Preen, who ran it from c1863 until its closure c1875, seems to have been a lessee."

Field Farm, Leebotwood.

Later census records (1861 onwards) show that the family occupied two households in Leebotwood. One was the grocer's shop in Leebotwood itself (the occupier always includes "grocer" among his professions) and the other a farm at the "Old Field" in Leebotwood (also the colliery). Since the two locations are very close, it may be a matter of chance who occupies which place in any given census.

The date of 1842 over the door of Field Farm suggests that although the rebuilding may have started "shortly before 1832" the present building was probably not completed until 1842.

In the 1861 census, two of Richard's sons were living in "Old Field, Leebotwood" and if this was the house occupied by manager and lessee of the colliery, then it suggests that Richard was running the colliery in 1861. Richard and Sarah and the rest of the family were still living in the shop.

By 1871 the position was reversed, with most of the family at the Old Field and only William in the grocer's shop.

In 1881, after William's death, Richard was alone in the grocer's shop while Sarah and the most of the family occupied the Old Field.

"Sarah Preen of the Field" died in 1881 and was buried in Leebotwood churchyard on 22nd December 1881.

Her gravestone has the inscription: "In loving memory of SARAH the beloved wife of RICHARD PREEN of LEEBOTWOOD who died on December 18th 1881 aged 68 years".

"Richard Preen of the Field" died in 1887 and was buried in Leebotwood churchyard on 1st December 1887.

His inscription is on the bottom of his wife's gravestone and reads: "Also in loving remembrance of RICHARD PREEN of LEEBOTWOOD who died on Novr 20th 1887 aged 79 years".

The picture shows the gravestone of Sarah and Richard Preen in Leebotwood church yard.

The **Calendar of Wills** contains the following entry: RICHARD PREEN, late of Leebotwood, Shropshire, grocer, farmer. Died 20th November 1887 at Leebotwood. Will proved Shrewsbury by Samuel Preen of Leebotwood, grocer & provisions dealer, son. Under £612-5-3d.

After Richard's death, his son John remained at Field Farm with his sister Mary and brother James while his youngest son Samuel took over the shop in Leebotwood.

Chapter Three: His Children & Grandchildren

3.1 William Preen 1842-1879

William Preen, the son of Richard Preen, shoemaker, and his wife Sarah (formerly King) was baptised in Cardington on 7th June 1842. (His elder brother, another William, only lived a few days since he was baptised on 29th April 1841 and buried on 3rd May 1841.) At this time, the family were living at Enchmarsh and Richard was working as a shoemaker. By July 1844, the family had moved to Leebotwood and his father was described as a "shop keeper".

The house which was once the grocer's shop is shown on the right of the picture, and the Copper Kettle is a later addition.

In 1851 William was living with the rest of the family in the grocer's shop in Leebotwood.

In 1861, William and his younger brother James were living in the Old Field and William was described as a farmer's son.

In 1871 he was by himself and working as a grocer in Leebotwood while the rest of the family were at the Old Field.

William Preen died on 28th November 1879 at the Field, Leebotwood. He was a grocer aged 37 years and the cause of death was given as "morbus corbes, morbus Brightii". The death was reported by Rebecca Bearman (illiterate) on 29th November

William Preen of the Field was buried in Leebotwood churchyard on 1st December 1879. His gravestone is in Leebotwood churchyard and bears the inscription: "In Loving Remembrance of WILLIAM Eldest Son of Richard and Sarah Preen of LEEBOTWOOD who died November 28th 1879 aged 37 years".

3.2 Annie Hughes (born Preen) 1844-1931

Anne Preen, the eldest daughter of Richard Preen and Sarah (born King) was born in Leebotwood in July 1844 and baptised in there on 21st July 1844.

In 1851 she was living with the rest of the family in the grocer's shop in Leebotwood. In 1861 she was probably also there but her name was given as "Jane" in the census.

She was married in Leebotwood church on 23rd May 1867. She was described as **Ann Preen**, a spinster of full age (actually 23) and living at Leebotwood, the daughter of Richard Preen, farmer. Her groom was **Christopher Hughes**, a bachelor of full age (actually 25), a compositor in a printing office and living in St Chads parish in Shrewsbury. His father was John Hughes, the Chief Constable of Shrewsbury.

```
                              |-Arthur John Hughes 1868-?
                              |-Edith Sarah Hughes 1870-?
                              |         mar 1898 ------- 3 children
                              | James D. Hinksman 1869-?
Anne Preen 1845-1931          |-Elizabeth Hughes 1876-?
       mar 1867 -----------|-Annie Gertrude Hughes 1878-?
Christopher Hughes            |-Mary Emily Hughes 1879-?
1842-1895                     |         mar 1905 --------- 2 children
                              | George Powell Hughes 1874-?
                              |-Christopher Charles Hughes 1881-?
                              |         mar 1910 --------- 1 child
                              | Florence Margaretta Duggan 1888-?
                              |-Elizabeth Mabel Grace Hughes 1882-?
                              |-Frances Dora Hughes 1886-? mar 1911
```

Their son Arthur John Hughes was born in the first quarter of 1868 in the Church Stretton district (possibly Leebotwood) and their daughter Edith Sarah Hughes was born there in the first quarter of 1870.

In 1871, Anne and Christopher and their two children were staying with Anne's parents in the grocer's shop in Leebotwood. Fred Medlicott (the grandson of Anne's sister Mary) said that they had four other children, Christopher, Gertrude, Dora and Mary.

Number 18 Market Square where Annie Hughes lived.

In 1881, Christopher and Annie Hughes were living in Market Square, Bishops Castle and Christopher was a printer. With them were six children, Arthur (aged 13), Edith (aged 11), Elizabeth (aged 4), Annie (aged 3), Mary (aged 1) and Christopher (aged 1 month). Also present were a servant and a nurse.

In 1891, Christopher and Annie Hughes were still living in No 18 Market Square, Bishops Castle and Christopher was now a "job printer and stationer". With them were six of their children, Ethel (aged 14 who may have been registered as "Elizabeth"), Annie (aged 13), Mary (aged 11), Christopher (aged 10), Elizabeth (aged 8) and Frances (aged 4). Arthur John Hughes (aged 23 & born in Leebotwood) was boarding at 69 Abbey Street, Derby and working as a printer's manager. Edith Sarah Hughes (aged 21 and born in Shrewsbury) was living at 10 Palatine Road, Withington as a companion to Elizabeth Beaulah aged 77.

Christopher Hughes died in the summer of 1895, aged 54, and was buried in Bishops Castle on 16 April 1895.

Annie continued to run the shop after his death.

In 1901 Annie Hughes was living in The Square, Bishops Castle and was a "printer and stationer". With her were three of her daughters (Mary aged 21, Mabel (aged 18 and a pupil teacher in a board school) and Dora aged 14) and her son Christopher (a printer/compositor aged 20). Arthur John Hughes (now aged 33) may have been the "Arthur Hughes aged 36 & born in Wem" who was a boarder in the household of Thomas Warall in 11 Skinner Street, Birmingham and worked as a printer's compositor. Edith Sarah had married James Hincksman in 1898 and they were living in Welsh Street, Bishops Castle with their daughter Dorothy. Annie Gertrude Hughes (now aged 23) appeared as "Annie Hughes" and was a probationer nurse in the Infirmary in Carlisle. Elizabeth Hughes (possibly also called "Ethel M Hughes" and now aged 25) has not yet been found.

In 1911, Annie Hughes (now 66) was still working as a stationer at 18 Market Square, Bishops Castle. Her daughter Mabel (now 28) was living with her and working as a head teacher in an elementary school. There was also a shop assistant, Mildred Prosser, living in the household. The rest of the family had left home by now. Arthur John Hughes (now 43) has not been found. Ethel Sarah was living in High St, Bishops Castle with her husband James Hinksman and their three children. Elizabeth (now 35) has not been found. Gertrude was living in Brixworth, Northants and working as a sick nurse. Mary Emily was living in Albrighton with her husband George Powell Hughes and their two children. Christopher was living in Rhyader with his wife and daughter and working as a printer and stationer. Dora (now 24) has not been found.

ANNIE HUGHES,
of Pleasant Cottage, Llandrindod Wells.

Widow of Christopher Hughes, of The Square, Bishop's Castle, and formerly resident at that address for fifty years.

On 23 November 1931, Annie Hughes, aged 87, was buried in Bishops Castle. Her address was Pleasant Cottage, Llandrindod Wells which suggests that she had retired from running her stationers shop and moved to live near her younger son Christopher Charles Hughes and his family.

ANNIE'S CHILDREN

Fred Medlicott, grandson of Annie's sister Mary, remembered six children, Arthur, Edith, Christopher, Gertrude, Dora and Mary.

Arthur John Hughes 1868-?

Arthur John Hughes was born in the first quarter of 1868 in the Church Stretton district. In 1871, he and his family were staying with his grandparents in Leebotwood. By 1881, the family had moved to Market Square, Bishops Castle and Arthur (aged 13) was at home with his family. In 1891, Arthur John Hughes (aged 23 & born in Leebotwood) was boarding at 69 Abbey Street, Derby and working as a printer's manager. In 1901, Arthur John Hughes (now aged 33) may have been the "Arthur Hughes aged 36 & born in Wem" who was a boarder in the household of Thomas Warall in 11 Skinner Street, Birmingham and worked as a printer's compositor. By 1911, Arthur John Hughes (now 43) has not been found.

Edith Sarah Hughes later Hinksman 1870-1923

Edith Sarah Hughes was born in the Church Stretton district (possibly Leebotwood) in the first quarter of 1870. In 1871, she and her family were staying with her grandparents in Leebotwood. By 1881, the family had moved to Market Square, Bishops Castle and Edith (aged 11) was at home with her family. In 1891, Edith Sarah Hughes (aged 21 and born in Shrewsbury) was living at 10 Palatine Road, Withington as a companion to Elizabeth Beaulah aged 77.

In the summer of 1898, Edith Sarah Hughes married James Downes Hinksman in the Clun registration district and in 1901 James and Edith Hinksman were living in Welsh Street, Bishops Castle with their daughter Dorothy (aged 1). James was a saddle and harness maker. In 1911, James and Edith Hinksman were living at 40 High Street, Bishops Castle and James was a poultry dealer. With them were three children (Dorothy aged 11, Evelyn aged 6 and James aged 2) and a servant Agnes M Wyatt aged 18. Although the family seem to have been living in Bishops Castle, baptisms of the children have not been found in the registers.

On 24 January 1923, Edith Sarah Hinksman of 6 Bull Street, Bishops Castle was buried.

Elizabeth Hughes 1876-?

Elizabeth Hughes was born in the first quarter of 1876 in the Clun registration district and in 1881 Elizabeth aged 4 was living in Marker Square, Bishops Castle with her parents. The family was still there in 1891 and included a daughter "Ethel M. Hughes" aged 14. She has not been found after this.

Annie Gertrude Hughes 1878-1966

Anne Gertrude Hughes was born in the Clun registration district in the second quarter of 1878. In 1881, Annie (aged 3) was living at home with her family in Market Square, Bishops Castle and she was still there in 1891 (aged 13). In 1901 Annie Gertrude Hughes (now aged 23) appeared as "Annie Hughes" and was a probationer nurse in the Infirmary in Carlisle. In 1911 Gertrude Hughes (aged 33) was living in Northampton Road, Brixworth in the household of Abraham Edlred, farmer, and working as a sick nurse.

Mary Emily Hughes 1879-?

Mary Emily Hughes was born in the Clun registration district in the last quarter of 1879. In 1881, Mary (aged 1) was living at home with her family in Market Square, Bishops Castle and she was still there in 1891 (aged 11). Her father died in 1895 and in 1901, Mary (aged 21) was living in Bishops Castle with her mother and sisters. In the third quarter of 1905, Mary Emily Hughes married George Powell Hughes in the Clun District (the marriage has not been found in the Bishops Castle register). In 1911, George Powell Hughes from Lydbury North and Mary Emily Hughes from Bishops Castle were living at Lower Wood Farm in Albrighton and George was a farmer and coal merchant. The household included their son Francis Clifford Hughes aged 4 and their daughter Margaret Joyce Hughes aged 2.

Christopher Charles Hughes 1881-1953

Christopher Charles Hughes was born in the Clun registration district in the second quarter of 1881. In 1881, Christopher (aged 1 month) was living at home with his family in Market Square, Bishops Castle and he was still there in 1891 (aged 10). His father died in 1895 and in 1901, Christopher (a printer/compositor aged 20) was living in Bishops Castle with his mother and sisters. He married Florence Margaretta Duggan in the Rhyader district in the first quarter of 1910 and in 1911 He was living in Rhyader with his wife and daughter and working as a printer and stationer.

Elizabeth Mabel Grace Hughes, later Downes 1882-?

Elizabeth Mabel Grace Hughes was born in the Clun registration district in the last quarter of 1882. In 1891, Elizabeth (aged 8) was living at home with her family in Market Square, Bishops Castle. In 1901, Mabel (aged 18 and a pupil teacher in a board school) was living in Bishops Castle with her family. In 1911, Mabel (now 28) was living with her mother and working as a head teacher in an elementary school. In the last quarter of 1914 she marred Edward J. Downes in the Clun district. Their children were probably born in Wrexham and Atcham.

Frances Dora Hughes 1886-1979

Frances Dora Hughes was born in the Clun registration district in the last quarter of 1886. In 1891, Frances (aged 4) was living at home with her family in Market Square. In 1901, Dora aged 14 was living at home in Bishops Castle with her mother and family. She has not been found in 1911. She may have died in Oswestry in the second quarter of 1979.

3.3 James Preen 1846- 1927

James Preen, the son of Richard Preen, shopkeeper, and Sarah (formerly King) was born in Leebotwood in 1846 and baptised there on 10th September 1846.

In 1851 he was living with the rest of the family in the grocer's shop in Leebotwood, but in 1861 he was living at the Old Field with his elder brother William. In 1871 he was back in the grocer's shop with most of the family.

After this, he seems to have left Leebotwood for a while and obtained employment with the railways.

```
                              |-Sarah Jane Preen 1873-1877
                              |-William Preen 1874-1957
                              |          mar 1898 ----------- 2 children
James Preen 1846-1927         | Rhoda Christine Morris c1874-1961
mar 1871          ----------- |-Richard Preen 1876-1877
Eliza Jones c1848-1885        |-John Arthur Preen 1882-1882
```

On 17th December 1871, James was married in the Parish church at Liverpool. He was described as **James Preen** a bachelor of full age and a railway porter living at Orphan Street and the son of Richard Preen farmer. His bride was **Eliza Jones** a spinster of full age living at Orphan Street and the daughter of Evan Jones joiner.

1873: Their daughter **Sarah Jane Preen** was born in the first quarter of 1873 in the Bolton district and was buried in Leebotwood on 5th February 1877.

She is included on the gravestone for the family of Evan Jones her grandfather in Leebotwood churchyard with the inscription: "In Loving Memory of SARAH JANE daughter of JAMES & ELIZA PREEN who died January 31st 1877 aged 4 years.

1874: Their son **William Preen** was born on 1st October 1874 and grew up and outlived his parents. He is discussed below.

1876: Their son **Richard Preen** was born on 12th September 1876 at 38 Hopkins Street, Tonge-with-Haulgh. His parents were James Preen, pointsman on a railway, and Eliza (formerly Jones). The birth was registered on 18th October by his father. **Richard** Preen died on 21st September 1877 at 10 Ebenezer St, Tranmere. He was aged 12 months, and the son of James Preen a railway signalman and the cause of death was "congestion of the lungs". The death was reported on 22nd September by his father.

In the 1881 census James and Eliza were living at Tranmere in Cheshire and James was working as a railway signalman and accompanied by his wife Eliza and their son William.

1882: Their son **John Arthur Preen** was born on 6th November 1882 at 6 Clyde St, Tranmere. His parents were James Preen, a railway signalman, and Eliza (Jones). The birth was registered on 8th November by Margaret Disley of the same address. He died soon afterwards.

Their two youngest sons were born in Cheshire and both died in infancy. James' wife died in the autumn of 1885 and after this, James returned to the family home in Leebotwood.

In 1891, James Preen was widowed and living at Field House, Leebotwood with his brother John and sister Mary.

James was still living at The Field in 1901 and 1911. In 1901, Drusilla or Priscilla Hince from Aston Munslow was boarding at the farm and in 1911, after the death of his sister Mary, she was working as the housekeeper.

On 12th February 1927, James Preen of Field Farm, aged 80 years, was buried in Leebotwood.

William Preen 1874-1957

Their son **William Preen** was born on 1st October 1874 at 34 Spring Field, Tonge-with-Haulgh. His parents were James Preen, pointsman on a railway, and Eliza (formerly Jones). The birth was registered on 3rd November by his father.

In 1881 he was living at home with his parents. Following his mother's death in 1885, William and his father returned to Leebotwood.

William Preen, aged 16, and born in Bolton Lancashire, was apprenticed to a blacksmith in Smethcott in the 1891 census.

In 1898, **William Preen** of Longsight married **Rhoda Christine Morris** of Catstree in St Peters Church at Worfield and moved to Manchester where William worked as a farrier and shoeing smith.

In 1901 they were living in Manchester with their son Thomas John, born in 1900.

In 1911 they were still living in Manchester and they had a second son James Walter, born in 1902.

William died in Manchester in 1957 and his widow Rhoda died there in 1961.

3.4 Mary Medlicott (born Preen) 1848 - 1908

Mary Preen was the daughter of Richard Preene, shopkeeper, and his wife Sarah (born King). She was born in Leebotwood in the last quarter of 1848 and was baptised there on 17th September.

In the 1851 census, Mary Preen aged 2 was living in Leebotwood with the rest of her family.

In 1861, Mary Preen (aged 12 and born in Leebotwood) was boarding in a school in Claremont Bank, Shrewsbury.

On the marriage certificate it states: "On 25th June 1868, she was married in the Primitive Methodist chapel in Castle Court, Shrewsbury. She was described as **Mary Preen** a spinster aged 20 and a grocer's daughter living at Leebotwood and the daughter of Richard Preen grocer. Her groom was **William Medlicott** a bachelor aged 27 and a railway signalman living at Leemor Common Wistanstow and the son of John Medlicott miller."

```
                               |-Percy Ernest Medlicott 1870-1871
                               |-Mary Preen Medlicott 1872-?
Mary Preen 1848-1908           |        mar 1895 -------- 4 children
       mar 1868 ----------- |   Richard Jervis
William Medlicott 1841-?     |-William Edward Medlicott 1873-1875
                             |-Arthur John Medlicott 1876-?
                             |        mar 1914 -------- 5 children
                             | Ethel M. Charles
```

In the 1871 census, William and Mary Medlicott were living at The Corner, Wistanstow with their baby son Ernest Percy and William was working as a railway signalman.

Mary's grandson Fred Medlicott said she married a *"William Medlicott of Wentnor and had other children who died in infancy as well as the two who appeared in the 1881 census. William Medlicott went abroad c1877 to, I believe, New Zealand. After a time he stopped writing when his wife was persuaded not to continue answering his letters. She and the children went back to live at the Field in Leebotwood."* At present (2012) the journey to New Zealand cannot be checked because the passenger lists are only available after 1890.

In the 1881 census, Mary was at Field House under her married name of Medlicott and accompanied by two children, Mary Preen Medlicott (age 9) and Arthur John Medlicott (age 5).

In 1891 she and her son Arthur were living at Field House with two of her brothers.

In 1901, Mary was still at Field House with her two brothers.

Mary Medlicott died in 1908 at the age of 59 and was buried in Leebotwood on 13th March 1908.

HER CHILDREN

Mary Preen Medlicott, later Jarvis 1872-?

Mary Preen Medlicott was born in 1871 in the Church Stretton registration district. In the 1881 census she was living with her mother at Field House in Leebotwood. In 1891 she was working as a servant in 21 Greek St, Southport in the household of George Carter a Major in the Salvation Army.

In the winter of 1895, Mary married Richard Jervis and in 1901, Richard and Mary Jervis were living in the Keepers House, Kelmarsh, Northants with their daughter Dorothy and Richard was working as a gamekeeper.

In 1911, Richard and Mary Jervis were living at Albrightlee Cottage, Battlefield, Shrewsbury and Richard was working as an estate waggoner. They now had four children, a daughter and three sons.

Arthur John Medlicott 1876-?

Arthur John Medlicott was born in 1875 in the Church Stretton registration district and in both 1881 and 1891 he was living with his mother in Field House, Leebotwood.

In 1901 Arthur was boarding at Burnhill Green, Patshull, Staffs in the household of Stephen Chapman and working as a carpenter.

In 1911 Arthur Medlicott was living in High St, Watlington, Oxfordshire and working as a carpenter.

He married Ethel Charles in 1914 and they moved to Birmingham where their five children were born.

3.5 John Preen 1851-1929

John Preen, the son of Richard Preen and Sarah (formerly King) was born at Leebotwood in the third quarter of 1851 and baptised on Christmas Day.

Field Farm, Leebotwood.

In 1861 and 1871, John was living with his family in the grocer's shop. From 1881 onwards, John was living at Field Farm and working as a farmer.

After his father's death in 1887, John Preen appeared as head of the household in Field Farm.

In 1891, John Preen (an unmarried farmer) was head of the household and was accompanied by his widowed brother James, his sister Mary Medlicott and his nephew Arthur Medlicott.

In 1901, John, James and Mary were still living there and they also had a boarder, Drusilla or Priscilla Hince from Aston Munslow.

Fred Medlicott (Mary's grandson) said of John that *"he farmed at the Fields until his death in 1929".*

In 1911, after Mary's death, John and James were still at Field Farm and Priscilla Hince was now working as the housekeeper.

James died in February 1927 and was buried in Leebotwood and John continued with the farm.

John Preen of Field Farm was buried at Leebotwood on 23rd September 1929.

3.6 Richard Preen 1854-1925

Richard Preen, the son of Richard Preen and Sarah King, was born in Leebotwood in 1854 and appeared in the 1861 census with the majority of the family in the grocer's shop. He did not appear again in the Leebotwood records.

He seems to have become a cabinet maker and probably left home when he became an apprentice. In 1871, he was lodging in Shrewsbury and was described as a "cabinet maker's apprentice". No details of his apprenticeship have yet been found.

The marriage was held on 24th February 1880 at the Wesley chapel, Withington near Chorlton in Lancashire, by certificate according to the rites and ceremonies of the Wesleyan Methodists. The groom was **Richard Preen**, a bachelor aged 26 and a cabinetmaker, living at 29 Spring Gardens Northampton and the son of Richard Preen, grocer. The bride was **Martha Jane Cheesbrough**, (shown in the picture supplied by her great-grand-daughter Jane Taylor) a spinster aged 20, living at Beulah Lodge Withington and the daughter of George Cheesbrough, grocer. The witnesses were Joseph O'Gorman (registrar), Samuel Deakin and Ann Elizabeth Cheesbrough and all five signed.

The 1881 census showed him living in Northampton and working as a cabinet maker. He was married to Martha Jane and they had a baby daughter, Annie Lilian, who had been born in Northampton. Martha herself had been born in Manchester while Martha's mother had been born in Newbald, Yorkshire.

```
                      |-Annie Lilian Preen 1881-? mar 1913 Maurice Williams
                      |-Elizabeth Emily Preen 1883-? mar 1912 Herbert Monk
                      |-Frederick William Preen 1885-1955
Richard Preen         |        mar 1915 -----------|-Barbara Preen 1917-?
1854-1925             | Elizabeth Davies           |-Margaret Preen 1925-?
mar 1880 ----------   |-Edith Martha Preen 1887-?
Martha Jane           |
Cheesbrough           |-Richard Harold Preen 1889-1890
c1860-1923            |-Albert Cecil Preen 1891-?
                      |        mar 1923 -----------|-Beryl Preen 1925-?
                      | Beatrice H. Davies
```

By July 1883, the family had moved to Withington and by September 1885 they had moved to 89 Wilmslow Road, Withington. They were still there in August 1887 and August 1891.

Their daughter **Elizabeth Emily Preen** was born on 27th July 1883 at Oak Bank building, Withington. Her parents were Richard Preen, cabinet maker, and Martha Jane (formerly Cheeseborough) and the birth was registered by her father on 7th September. She was probably married in 1912 to Herbert E. Monk.

Their son, **Frederick William Preen** was born at 89 Wilmslow Road, Withington on 24th September 1885. His parents were Richard Preen, a cabinet maker, and Martha Jane (Cheesbrough). The birth was registered on 5th November by his father

Their daughter, **Edith Martha Preen** was born on 24th August 1887 at 89 Wilmslow Road, Withington. Her parents were Richard Preen, a cabinet maker, and Martha Jane (Cheesbrough). The birth was registered on 5th October by her father.

Their son **Richard Harold Preen** was born on 14th April 1889 at 89 Wilmslow Road, Withington. His parents were Richard Preen, a master cabinet maker, & Martha Jane (formerly Cheesborough) and the birth was registered by his father on 24th May. He died soon afterwards

In the 1891 census, the family were living at 89 Wilmslow Road, Withington and Richard was a cabinet maker.

Their son, **Albert Cecil Preen** was born on 22nd August 1891 at 89 Wilmslow Road, Withington. His parents were Richard Preen, a cabinet maker, and Martha Jane (Cheesbrough). The birth was registered on 8th October by his father.

In the 1901 census, they were living at 9 Davenport Avenue, Wilmslow. Richard was a cabinet maker and his son Frederick (aged 15) was a cabinet maker's apprentice. Annie (aged 20) was a telegraph and counter clerk and her sister Elizabeth (aged 17) was a telephone operator.

In 1911, they were living at 105 Wilmslow Road, Withington, Richard and his son Frederick were cabinet makers and Albert Cecil (now 19) was an apprentice cabinet maker. All three daughters were working for S.C. & T.

The Calendar of Wills shows that Martha Jane Preen died on 21st March 1923 at 106 Wilmslow Road, Withington and probate was granted on 14th April 1923.

Richard Preen died on 31st October 1925 at 106 Wilmslow Road, Withington and probate was granted on 30th November 1925 to Frederick and Albert (cabinet makers) and Edith Martha (spinster).

THEIR CHILDREN

Annie Lilian Preen, later Williams 1881-?

Annie Lilian was the eldest child of Richard and Martha Jane Preen and was born in Northampton. She accompanied them to Wilmslow Road, Withington and grew up there. In 1901 she was living at home with her parents and working as a telegraph and counter clerk She married Maurice Williams in 1913.

Elizabeth Emily Preen, later Monk 1883-?

Their daughter Elizabeth Emily Preen was born on 27th July 1883 at Oak Bank building, Withington. Her parents were Richard Preen, cabinet maker, and Martha Jane (formerly Cheeseborough) and the birth was registered by her father on 7th September. In 1901 she was living at home with her parents and working as a telephone operator. In 1912 she married Herbert E. Monk.

Frederick William Preen 1885-1955

Their son, **Frederick William Preen** was born at 89 Wilmslow Road, Withington on 24th September 1885. His parents were Richard Preen, a cabinet maker, and Martha Jane (Cheesbrough). The birth was registered on 5th November by his father. He was living at home with his parents in both 1891 and 1901 and in 1901 he was a cabinet maker's apprentice. In 1911 he was still living at home and was now a cabinet maker like his father. In 1915, Frederick married Elizabeth Davies and their daughter Barbara was born in 1917. Their daughter Margaret was born in 1925.

Edith Martha Preen 1887-1969

Their daughter, **Edith Martha Preen** was born on 24th August 1887 at 89 Wilmslow Road, Withington. Her parents were Richard Preen, a cabinet maker, and Martha Jane (Cheesbrough). The birth was registered on 5th October by her father. She lived at home with her family until her father's death in 1925. She never married and died in the third quarter of 1969 in Aled, Denbighshire.

Albert Cecil Preen 1891-?

Albert Cecil Preen was born on 22nd August 1891 at 89 Wilmslow Road, Withington. His parents were Richard Preen, a cabinet maker, and Martha Jane (Cheesbrough). The birth was registered on 8th October by his father. In 1901 and 1911 he was living at home with his family and by 1911 he was an apprentice cabinet maker. In 1923, Albert Cecil married Beatrice Handel Davies. **Beryl Preen** was born on 9th April 1925 at 14 Claremount Grove, Didsbury. She was the daughter of Albert Cecil Preen, a cabinet maker, and Beatrice Handel (formerly Davies) and her birth was registered on 1st May by her father.

The Village Shop run by Samuel was in the house on the right.
The Copper Kettle is a later addition.

3.7 Samuel Preen 1856 - 1938

Samuel Preen was born on 26th July 1856 at Leebotwood. His parents were Richard Preen, a draper & grocer, and Sarah (King). The birth was registered on 5th September by his father.

In the 1861 census, Samuel aged 4 was in Leebotwood with his family.

In 1871, his eldest brother William was at the shop while the rest of the family were living at The Field. Samuel (aged 14) was working as a farm labourer along with his three elder brothers.

In 1881, Samuel (now aged 24) was living at Field House, Leebotwood with other members of his family.

When his brother John took over the tenancy of Field Farm following their father's death in 1887, he left Samuel to take on the grocery business and Samuel decided he needed a wife to help him run the business.

Samuel Preen 1856-1938	|-Arthur Frank Preen 1890-1960
mar 1888 ----------------------	|-Agnes Annie Preen 1891-1984
Ellen Matthews 1859-1940	|-Edith Nellie Preen 1894-1926

Thomas Matthews of Smethcott had four daughters (Ellen, Annie, Jane and Agnes) and it was said that Samuel Preen wanted to marry the youngest, but her father said the eldest must be married first so Samuel agreed to marry her instead.

Smethcott Church

Back in 1881, John Wilks had been living at Pool House, Smethcott with his sister Jane Matthews, her husband Thomas Matthews and three of their children (Ann aged 16, James aged 12 and Agnes aged 9). This means that Agnes would have been 16 in 1888 and would have needed her father's permission to marry. In 1881 Ellen (aged 21) was working as a housemaid in Smethcott Vicarage and Jane (aged 14) was a boarder at the National School in Smethcott.

The marriage took place in Smethcott on 3rd October 1888. The groom was **Samuel Preen**, a bachelor of full age, a grocer living in Leebotwood and the son of Richard Preen, grocer. His bride was **Ellen Matthews**, a spinster of full age living in Smethcott and the daughter of Thomas Matthews, the parish clerk. Although they were married in early October, it was said to have been snowing on their wedding day.

1890: Arthur Frank Preen was born on 21st September 1890. He was at home with his parents in Leebotwood in 1891. Arthur was educated at a private school in Church Stretton and his two sisters were also well educated. In 1901, he and his sisters were living in Smethcott with his aunt Annie Matthews, who was head of the household. In 1911, Arthur Frank Preen (aged 20) was now a farmer and head of the household in Smethcott while his aunt Annie Matthews was there as a housekeeper. There were also three live-in servants.

In the 1891 census, Samuel and Ellen Preen were living in Leebotwood with their six-month-old son Arthur Frank Preen. Samuel was described as a grocer. Meanwhile in Smethcott, the head of the household was still John Wilkes a rabbit-catcher aged 71. Living with him were his brother-in-law and sister, Thomas and Jane Matthews, and three of their children (John aged 34, James aged 29 and Agnes aged 19).

1891: Agnes Annie Preen was born on 26th November 1891 and in the 1901 census she was living in Smethcott with her aunt Annie Matthews. In 1911, she was living in the grocer's shop in Leebotwood with her parents and attending school.

1894: Edith Nellie Preen was born in 1894 and in the 1901 census she was living in Smethcott with her aunt Annie Matthews. In 1911, she was living in the grocer's shop in Leebotwood with her parents and attending school.

In the 1901 census, Samuel and Ellen were living in Leebotwood with Ellen's sister Jane (aged 34) and brother James (aged 32). All four were described as grocers. In Smethcott, Annie Matthews was now the head of the household and with her were Samuel and Ellen's three children (Arthur aged 10, Agnes aged 9 and Annie aged 6).

In the 1911 census, Samuel and Ellen were still living in Leebotwood and running the grocer's shop. Agnes (aged 19) and Edith (aged 16) were living were living with them and attending school. Ellen's sister Jane (aged 44) and brother James (aged 42) were still there and working in the business. In Smethcott, Arthur Frank Preen (aged 20) was now a farmer and head of the household while his aunt Annie Matthews was there as a housekeeper. There were also three live-in servants.

Samuel and Ellen continued to run the shop and also expanded the business to include a corn merchants. The shop had a bakehouse in the kitchen and they also had a horse and trap with a large sign "Grocer and Baker" attached to the trap.

Site of Broadstead with the Copper Kitchen on the right

They also owned a small cottage nearby and the yard behind both shop and cottage.

Arthur Frank Preen served in the first world war (1914-1918) and this may have been when the farm in Smethcott was sold to the Cooksons. When Arthur returned home after the war, he farmed at Netley Hall Farm in Stapleton. .

In the late 1920s, a new house called "Broadstead") was built. The Preen family moved into Broadstead and the shop was sold to Mr Morgan of Cardington (brother to the Lewis Morgan who kept the shop in Cardington and had married Adelaide Preen, Samuel's cousin once removed).

In 1930, the shop was sold to Samuel Beamond and the Beamond family lived there and ran the shop for many years. The Preens continued with the corn merchant's business. In the spring of 1938, Samuel Preen died and in 1940 his widow Ellen died. Ellen Preen of Broadstead was buried in Smethcott churchyard on 19th January 1940. On 26th October 1949, her sister Ann Matthews of Broadstead was buried there too.

Because of their connections with the Matthews family, Samuel and his children were buried in Smethcott churchyard whereas the rest of these Preens were buried in Leebotwood.

THEIR CHILDREN

Arthur Frank Preen 1890-1960

Arthur Frank Preen was born on 21st September 1890. He was at home with his parents in Leebotwood in 1891. Arthur was educated at a private school in Church Stretton and his two sisters were also well educated. In 1901, he and his sisters were living in Smethcott with his aunt Annie Matthews, who was head of the household. In 1911, Arthur Frank Preen (aged 20) was now a farmer and head of the household in Smethcott while his aunt Annie Matthews was there as a housekeeper. There were also three live-in servants.

Arthur Frank Preen served in the first world war (1914-1918) and this may have been when the farm in Smethcott was sold to the Cooksons.

The picture, taken in 1955, shows Arthur standing next to the vicar after the blessing of the new Leebotwood vicarage.

When Arthur returned home after the war, he farmed at Netley Hall Farm in Stapleton. Arthur was not successful as a farmer because he neglected the farm to go hunting with the local vicar. He used the title "Major Preen" and behaved like a "gentleman farmer" rather than a working one.

In due course, the farm "went bust" and Arthur joined the rest of the family in Leebotwood. He continued as a corn merchant and was also a church warden in Leebotwood.

He continued to live in Broadstead after his mother's death in 1940. Arthur was remembered by his neighbours as a "pompous little man" who always had to do **something** to draw attention to himself during every church service. Arthur died on 8th May 1960 and was buried in Smethcott churchyard.

Agnes Annie Preen 1891-1984

Agnes Annie Preen was born on 26th November 1891 and in the 1901 census she was living in Smethcott with her aunt Annie Matthews. In 1911, she was living in the grocer's shop in Leebotwood with her parents and attending school. After the Preens sold the shop around 1930, Agnes taught at Coleham School.

Site of Broadstead

When Agnes Annie Preen retired from teaching, she lived at Broadstead and after Arthur's death on 8th May 1960, she continued to live there alone.

The Preen family was wealthy and the cottage at Broadstead was furnished with antique furniture, but Agnes lived until she was 92 and in her latter years the cost of her care left her impoverished.

She died on 1st September 1984 and was buried in Smethcott churchyard along with the rest of her family. Broadstead was pulled down because it was said to be in the way of a road-widening scheme and the contents were sold off or thrown away.

All that remains today is a gate in the fence by the main road and there is no evidence that the road-widening scheme was ever carried out.

Edith Nellie Preen 1894-1926

Edith Nellie Preen was born in 1894 and in the 1901 census she was living in Smethcott with her aunt Annie Matthews. In 1911, she was living in the grocer's shop in Leebotwood with her parents and attending school.

Edith Nellie Preen was living Netley Hall Farm in Stapleton when she died on 28th September 1926. She was said to have died of a broken heart because the family wouldn't let her marry Jack Shakeshaft, but there may have been another more immediate cause. She was buried in Smethcott churchyard on 4th October 1926, aged 32 years and is commemorated on the same gravestone as her parents.

Chapter Four: The 2012 Family Reunion

In June 2012, the Preen Family Reunion was held in Leebotwood Parish Hall. This lies on the main road, but, as this picture shows, it is almost invisible. In the centre of the picture you can see the bus stop (opposite the Pound Inn) and just to the left of it may be seen the roof of the Village Hall. In fact there is a large car park and a sizable hall once you find it.

Leebotwood Village Hall

This summer saw the publication of the first volume of the new "History of the Preen Family" which related to the Cardington Group and the Preens of Leebotwood were part of that group. This was released at the reunion and copies were on sale at the meeting.

The meeting followed the now traditional format, with talks and an AGM before lunch. The talk described the fortunes of the Leebotwood Preens, which had now been well researched with new information about Annie Hughes and her stationers shop in Bishops Castle, Richard Preen and his cabinet making business in Withington and Samuel Preen and the grocers shop in Leebotwood.

Book Launch at Preen Reunion 2012

Lunch was a buffet provided by the ladies of the Leebotwood W.I. and was much appreciated. In the afternoon, we all set out to view the places associated with the Preen family.

At this meeting we launched the first volume to be printed of the new "History of the Preen Family". This will be a four-volume book with Volume One describing the early history of the family (before 1660) and then a volume for each of the three groups.

Volume Two described the Cardington group from 1660 to 1911. Philip and Mary Preen are believed to be the common ancestors for this group and they first appear in the parish registers for Hope Bowdler in 1660. The 1911 census is the latest one to be available and so the history ends with those families who appeared in this census. The book may be bought at a family reunion or ordered from our website *www.preen.org.uk*

At the reunion this year we walked along the main road to view the site of the village shop, shown below. It is now a private residence and so we had to be content with looking at it from across the road.

Then we walked further along the road to look at the site of Broadstead Cottage, shown below.

We decided not to visit Field Farm but instead we returned to the Village Hall and then used cars to go and visit the church (shown below).

There were several gravestones commemorating this branch of the family in the churchyard at Leebotwood.

We found the gravestone for Richard and his wife Sarah and behind it that for their son William. They have a distinctive shape unlike the other gravestones around them.

We know from the registers that James, John and Mary were all buried in Leebotwood, and would have expected to find their gravestones in the newer part of the graveyard. We searched diligently but could find no trace of any memorial.

We did find the four-sided memorial (shown here) to Evan Jones and his family which included Sarah Jane Preen, daughter of James and Eliza. Her two younger brothers who died in infancy were not mentioned and were probably buried in Tranmere, Cheshire where they died. Although Eliza, James' wife, was the daughter of Evan Jones, she was not mentioned either.

Interior of Leebotwood Church

After looking round the graveyard, we went inside the church, where we were shown some of the original registers with the entries relating to the Preen family. We also admired the wall paintings, even though they have become rather worn with the passing of the centuries.

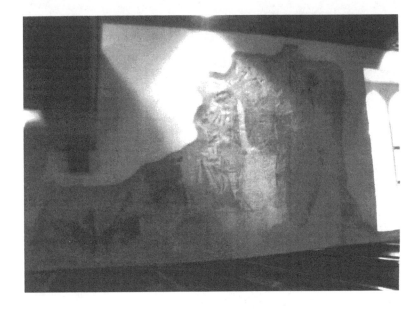

Some members also visited Smethcott church a few miles away where Samuel Preen and his family are buried.

The rest returned to the Village Hall to look at the family archives and enjoy tea.

Smethcott Church

Leebotwood Village Hall

PREEN FAMILY HISTORY STUDY GROUP
Minutes of the Annual General Meeting 2012

The above meeting took place at Leebotwood Village Hall on Sunday 10th June 2012 and the following committee members were present: -

Sue Laflin   -   Chairman, Editor & Archivist

Angela Clarke -   Treasurer & Secretary

Philip Davies   -   Publicity Officer

Bill Preen   -   Honorary Member

Also Present: Geoffrey O. Preen, Valerie Devonshire, Philip Preen, Pat Preen, Barry Kirtlan, Geoff Preen, Teresa Preen, Glenys Egan, Pauline Davies, Lesley Cotterill, Roy Cotterill, Marion Bytheway, Philip Bytheway, Kathleen Fuller, Shiela Flynn, James Clarke & Phil Barker.

1) Reviewed last years minutes

There were no objections and this was taken as a record.

2) Matters Arising

a. The Chairman confirmed that there were no volunteers to take over the sale of books.

b. Sue said ideas for future meetings would be welcomed.

c. Last year Sue had produced T-shirts commemorating the meeting. It would be possible to produce T-shirts again this year if there were a demand for them. No-one expressed a wish to order any.

d. We propose to hold the next meeting in Coalport Village Hall and the year after we are open for suggestions.

3) Election of Committee

Present Committee are prepared to continue. This was approved.

4) Secretary's Report

a. Increase in Postage – The Secretary requested, to help prevent excessive costs of postage, she was trying to get as many e mail addresses as possible and asked anyone who has one could they pass it on to us.

b. Angela agreed to bring copies of her xl sheets to the next AGM to demonstrate how we now send out Newsletters etc.

c. An acknowledgement was made of receipt of a donation cheque for £50 from Brian Johnston to the PFHSG.

Also acknowledged was an article printed in a local paper of a Preen who was praised for her charity work, this was passed on by Fred Simonds. Both items were passed round for the Group to see

5) Treasurer's Report.

a. A copy of Account entries for the year was passed round for everyone to see. The Treasurer explained all transactions on the Account.

b. The Treasurer reports that Sue (our Editor) has taken £700 out of the Account (although it is not yet showing) but she has also made a contribution of £700 herself to cover the cost of printing for 100 copies of the new Cardington Hardback Book.

6) Editor's Report

a. The Editor reported that it has taken two years to get the new Cardington Book into a fit state to be published.

b. The Editor stated that she would be 80 at the end of the decade and not likely to be starting on another four-volume book after that. She has tried to make this new volume of books the definitive description of the family to allow other people to build on that, which is why she went for a high quality hard back book and assumes this will be in use for the next 50 years. There is a minimum print of 100 copies and it is going to cost around £1200-£1300 to produce this quality.

If she were to pay half towards the Bridgnorth Volume we hope when she gets to the Kings Stanley Volume there will be enough in the account to cover the cost. After the Kings Stanley there will be the Early History Volume One, and she expects to have all four available by the end of the decade.

c. The Editor asked if the Members were in agreement with those aims – all agreed.

7) Archivist

a. They have got copies of these books in the Shropshire Archives. Sue also has the original paper copies she intends to add to the collection in the Archives. This collection has not been donated it remains the property of the PFHSG and is in the Archives on indefinite loan, which ought to protect them. Sue hopes this means that if they ever do not have enough room for them they would return them to us not just bin it.

8) Publicity Officer

a.   Photographs of the local Churches were taken ready to include in the PFHSG   Newsletter. The picture, taken in 1955, shows him standing next to the vicar after the blessing of the new Leebotwood vicarage.

b.   Press releases were sent out and examples of these were shown in local Newspapers, Magazines and a Family Tree Magazine. Philip explained how he asked some of his customers doing various events in other parts of the UK to include snippets 'Calling All Preens' in that area.

9) Any Other Business

It was put to the table that numbers were slightly down this year and did they want the meeting held on a Saturday or Sunday next year – Members voted that next years meeting would be on a Saturday not Sunday.

The Chairman confirmed this and that said it will be held on the second Saturday in June. (June 8th 2013).